Merry
Christmas
Love
Lila
Christmas 2001

PRESENTED TO:

_____

_____

FROM:

_____

_____

DATE:

_____

WHITER THAN SNOW

ISBN 1-56292-871-6
Copyright © 2001 by Roy Lessin

Published by Honor Books
P.O. Box 55388
Tulsa, Oklahoma 74155

Book Design by LJ Designs
Illustrations by Heather Solum

WHITER THAN SNOW

Written by Roy Lessin

Illustrated by Heather Solum

Honor Books
Tulsa, Oklahoma

This book is dedicated
to all those who
have allowed their
Heavenly Father to use them
to express His heart
of mercy, love,
grace, and encouragement
to the hearts of others.

"Come now,

let us reason together,"

says the LORD.

"Though your sins are like scarlet,

they shall be as white as snow;

though they are red as crimson,

they shall be like wool."

ISAIAH 1:18

Forget about the weather,

This one thing I know,

Your heart won't be happy

Until it's whiter than snow.

THE LITTLE WHITE PUPPY

A little girl received a new white puppy for Christmas. She loved the puppy with all her heart and played with it for hours every day. "You are so white," she would often tell the puppy. "You are whiter than anything in this entire house." One morning, the little girl woke to find that the ground outside was covered with freshly-fallen snow. With great delight, she put on her snowsuit and gloves, took her puppy in her arms, and ran outside to build a snowman. When she had finished her snowman, she sat back in the snow to admire her handiwork, while the little puppy scampered around nearby.

As she watched, her eyes lit up with a flash of revelation. "Why little puppy," she exclaimed, "compared to my snowman, you are not as white as I thought you were. My snowman is the whitest thing I have ever seen!"

This same principle is true in our lives. We may think our hearts are pure and white because of the good things we do or the nice things we say. But when we compare our "whiteness" to the purity of Jesus Christ, even the whitest heart cannot come close. Jesus is the only One who can truly make our hearts whiter than snow.

Wash me, and I will be whiter than snow.

PSALM 51:7

Happy is the person

Whose heart has been set free

Whose sins have been forgiven

And cast into the sea.

As far as the east is from the west,

so far has he removed

our transgressions from us.

PSALM 103:12

HAPPY TO BE FORGIVEN

When our sins are forgiven, it means that we have been justified. Justified means that we are set free from the guilt of all our past sins. It has been said that justified is another way of saying, "Just as if I'd never sinned." How good and kind and gracious God has been to us! Through the blood of Jesus Christ, He has healed us from the pain of our sins; He has comforted us from the sorrow of our sins; He has lifted us from the weight of our sins; and He has pardoned us from the judgement of our sins.

It's easy to see why a heart that is forgiven is a happy heart.

Justification means that there isn't

a charge against you.

Your sins are completely wiped out;

God says He puts them out of His memory.

—Dwight L. Moody

There is an eternal smile

on the heart

that has been forgiven.

Our God, no one is like you.

We are all that is left of your chosen people,

And you freely forgive our sin and guilt.

You don't stay angry forever;

You're glad to have pity.

MICAH 7:18 CEV

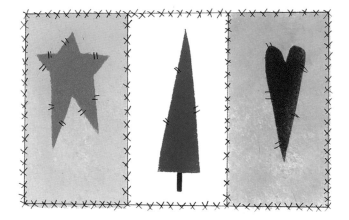

We pardon in the degree that we love.

—Frances De La Rochefoucauld

Blessed are they whose transgressions are forgiven,
whose sins are covered.
Blessed is the man whose sin
the Lord will never count against him.

Romans 4:7-8

The happiness that comes to us

when we are forgiven

is deeper and more intense

than any happiness

we have ever known before.

It is not a happiness based

on circumstances.

It is instead a happiness based

on the inward reality

of knowing that our hearts

are right with God.

Feelings come, and feelings go,

And feelings are deceiving;

My warrant is the Word of God—

Naught else is worth believing.

—W. M. CZAMANSKE

If we confess our sins, he is faithful and just

and will forgive us our sins and

purify us from all unrighteousness.

1 JOHN 1:9

Forgiveness not only delivers us

but it also shines a light

Having been justified by his grace,
we might become heirs
having the hope of eternal life.

TITUS 3:7

from the darkness of our past,
of hope upon our future.

If we walk in the light, as he is in the light,
we have fellowship with one another,
and the blood of Jesus, his Son, purifies us from all sin.

1 JOHN 1:7

When God forgives us

of our sins,

He also frees us

so that we are able

to forgive

the sins of others.

To forgive is to

set a prisoner free

and discover

the prisoner was you.

If you forgive men
when they sin against you,
your heavenly Father
will also forgive you.

MATTHEW 6:14

The Father sends us good gifts
Like softly falling snow,
Then blesses others through us
So other hearts can know.

When God's love fills your heart,
it will overflow with generosity.

The Perfect Time to Give

One day my wife and I had returned to our apartment from a Sunday church service. As I was about to place the key in the lock, my wife said, "I believe the Lord wants me to take a bag of groceries over to Jane's." Jane was a single parent with two young daughters, who lived a few doors down from us.

"The Lord told me to bring these to you," my wife said when Jane opened the door. "Please receive this gift from Him."

"You won't believe this," Jane responded. Her smile demonstrated her joy, even though her eyes were filled with tears." My girls and I were seated at the kitchen table when we heard your knock. I had just finished praying and thanking the Lord for our lunch, even though we had no food in the house. The Lord sent you here at the perfect time!

Give in such a way

that it will cause your heart

to break into a smile.

Each man should give what he has
decided in his heart to give,
not reluctantly or under compulsion,
for God loves a cheerful giver.

2 CORINTHIANS 9:7

From the fullness of his grace
we have all received one blessing after another.

JOHN 1:16

No matter how much God gives us in

the way of blessings,

His supply never runs dry, and His

arms are never empty,

for His heart is always full.

Do all the good you can,

to all the people you can,

in all the ways you can,

as often as ever you can,

as long as you can.

CHARLES SPURGEON

WE CAN NEVER OUT-GIVE GOD!

Give, and it will be given to you.

Scatter, and it will be returned to you.

Empty yourself, and you will be full.

Disperse, and you will gather again.

A heart filled with love
always has something to give.

In all things I have shown you

that by so toiling one must help the weak,

remembering the words of the

Lord Jesus, how he said,

"It is more blessed to give than to receive."

ACTS 20:35 RSV

Every man shall give as he is able, according to the blessing of the Lord your God which he has given you.

DEUTERONOMY 16:17 RSV

You can give without loving,
but you cannot love without giving.

AMY CARMICHAEL

Excel in this
grace of giving.
I am not commanding you,
but I want to test
the sincerity
of your love.

2 CORINTHIANS 8:7-8

The Lord is like a gentle wind

that blows upon my face,

To assure me of His presence

and cover me with grace.

A Refreshing Meal

A woman found herself embarrassed over her selection of dishes when company came. She had no complete set, only old mixed plates of various colors and styles. One day as she was struggling with this issue, she was reminded of a time when she once made a trip to a very poor part of a foreign country.

During her visit, she was invited into the home of a woman who lived in a tiny mud-brick house. There was no furniture to sit on, only bricks. The kitchen floor was made of dirt, and her stove consisted of a hole in the mud wall. The woman served a simple meal of eggs and handmade bread. The food was served on an old tin plate, yet the woman served the meal graciously and lovingly.

The woman radiated the love of Jesus in and through her to those she served. Everyone left her home refreshed and encouraged because God's presence was there, and He touched each one. Serving others has nothing to do with the color of the dishes. It has to do with how well you allow the wind of God's presence to refresh the hearts of your guests.

Refresh my heart in Christ.

PHILEMON 1:20

Each one should use whatever gift
he has received to serve others,
faithfully administering God's grace
in its various forms.

1 PETER 4:10

The greatest part of
loving is giving,
and the greatest
part of giving is to
give with joy.

Share with God's people
who are in need.
Practice hospitality.

ROMANS 12:13

Our path is clean
with sweeping,
The gate is open wide,
Who knows who may
be passing,
This way at eventide.

We lit our heart's bright candle;
Its beams shine far and clear
To tell one who may need it
That rest and love are here.

—Rachel Day

By all this we are encouraged.
In addition to our own encouragement,
we were especially delighted to
see how happy Titus was,
because his spirit has been refreshed
by all of you.

2 Corinthians 7:13

Blessed are the happiness makers;
Blessed are they that remove friction,
That make the courses of life smooth
And the converse of men gentle.

—Henry Ward Beecher

He who refreshes others

will himself be refreshed.

PROVERBS 11:25

Each day, we can express the heart of God

to the needs around us.

Like a cool, refreshing wind,

the love, mercy, and grace of God

can flow through us to others.

[Jesus said]:

"I tell you the truth,
whatever you did for one
of the least of these brothers
of mine, you did for me."

MATTHEW 25:40

God is strong and mighty

There's nothing He can't do

And in each storm and trial

His grace will bring us through.

Trusting God!

There are so many reasons why we can trust the Lord. One reason is that He is faithful. When I was facing major surgery, the Lord spoke these words to my heart, "I will hold your hand and walk through this with you." His words brought me instant comfort and assurance.

We can trust the Lord God because He is kind. I have never heard God speak an unkind or unloving word to me. He has never put me down, belittled me, or given up on me.

We can trust the Lord God because He is wise. When I have sought His counsel and guidance, He has never led me astray. His choices have always proved to be the best choices. I hate to think what my life would be like today if it were dependent upon my own wisdom.

We can trust the Lord because He is almighty. He has never failed me or made a mistake. I have seen Him change circumstances and people's hearts to bring to pass His will for my life.

We can trust God because He is Love. I have never had to earn His love, only receive it. He has loved me unconditionally. He wants only the highest good for my life. I can trust His love and give everything to Him because in His love, He gave everything to me.

The eternal God is

your refuge,

and underneath are the

everlasting arms.

DEUTERONOMY 33:27

The Lord will not fail you,

leave you, or ever let you down.

Nothing is impossible with God.

LUKE 1:37

Whatever your trial,

God sees.

Whatever your struggle,

God knows.

Whatever your cry,

God hears.

Whatever your difficulty,

God cares.

Whatever your problem,

God understands.

Whatever your need,

God provides.

The LORD is good,

a refuge in times of trouble.

He cares for those who trust in Him.

NAHUM 1:7

For each need, there is grace.

For each trial, there is grace.

For each task, there is grace.

For each step of obedience,

there is grace.

And for each circumstance

of life, there is grace.

Grace bears you up,
lifts you up,
and keeps you up.

Grace strengthens you,

empowers you,

enables you,

frees you,

equips you,

and motivates you.

Grace comes to you
freely and completely
by the good and
generous hand of God.
It comes to the
humble, the lowly,
the needy, and to all
who look to God alone.

[Jesus said]:

"My grace is sufficient for you,

for my power is made perfect in weakness."

2 CORINTHIANS 12:9

It's a happy face

Who knows God's grace

And hands it to another.

Who feels the refreshing Wind of God

Whenever storm clouds gather.